LIZZ

Illustrations by An

PUBLISHED BY STUDIO PUBLICATIONS (IPSWICH) LIMITED
32 PRINCES STREET, IPSWICH, SUFFOLK, ENGLAND

Lizzie Leek is one of the Munch Bunch.

She lives in a very pretty cooking-pot.

Lizzie is very good at cooking, sewing and knitting. She likes to make things for her friends.

One day Lizzie Leek invited her friends to her house for afternoon tea.

There was Pippa Pear, Emma Apple, Lucy Lemon and Sally Strawberry.

The sun was shining brightly, so they decided to sit in the garden.

The sun was very hot and Emma Apple became more and more rosy.

"Oh, you are lucky, Lizzie," Emma exclaimed, "having a big hat to shade you from the sun."

"We wish we had hats too," said Pippa and Sally together.

"Yes," said Lucy. "It would be nice to have a new hat for our garden fete next Sunday."

So Lizzie Leek decided to make a hat for each of her friends.

She collected lots of ribbons and flowers, and she even found an old sun-hat.

"This will make a very nice hat for Emma," she thought.

Lizzie was soon hard at work.

She stitched red ribbons and daisies on to the sun-hat she had made for Emma.

Then Lizzie made a red bonnet with a big daisy on one side for Pippa Pear; a lacy Spanish hat for Lucy Lemon, and a straw boater for Sally Strawberry.

At last the hats were ready. She carefully wrapped them in tissue paper and then put each of them into a hat box.

She then tied a label to each box, one for Pippa, one for Emma, one for Lucy, and one for Sally.

PIPPA
EMMA

The hats were ready to be delivered.

Just as Lizzie was wondering how to get the hats to her friends, Spud and Tom Tomato came to visit her.

"Perhaps Spud and Tom will deliver the hats for me," Lizzie thought to herself.

SALLY
PIPPA
EMMA

Spud and Tom agreed to help.

Off they went, each carrying two big boxes.

"Please hurry, because my friends want to wear their new hats at the garden fete this afternoon," Lizzie called after them.

Half-way to Emma's house they stopped for a rest.

"I've got a great idea," said Spud. "Let's swop all the labels around on the hat boxes."

"Oh yes," replied Tom. "Lucy Lemon will get Sally Strawberry's hat and Emma Apple will get Pippa Pear's hat. That will be fun."

Emma Apple was the first to open her box.

She was very disappointed.

Instead of a big sun-hat she had Pippa Pear's bonnet.

It didn't fit at all.

EMMA

Emma ran round to Pippa Pear's house, and found Pippa hidden under a huge sun-hat.

Pippa didn't know that she really had Emma's hat and Emma had her hat.

They decided to go and tell Lizzie Leek.

On the way to Lizzie Leek's house, Emma and Pippa met Lucy Lemon and Sally Strawberry.

Lucy's hat completely covered her eyes.

And Sally looked so silly in a lacy Spanish hat.

They didn't realise that Spud and Tom had swopped their labels around.

They all went to complain to Lizzie Leek.

Lizzie was horrified! "Spud and Tom must have changed the labels around," she said.

"Sally has got Lucy's hat on, and Lucy has got Sally's hat on. And Emma has got Pippa's hat on, and Pippa has got Emma's hat on.

Tom and Spud were hiding in the bushes, laughing.

They didn't notice Suzie Celery putting funny hats on their heads.

Lizzie Leek soon gave her friends the right hats.

They were all very pleased with their new hats.

As they were walking to the garden fete, Tom and Spud followed on behind.

They didn't know that they were wearing those funny hats.

And all day long, the rest of the Munch Bunch kept laughing at them.

Tom and Spud didn't know why, but we do, don't we?

Acknowledgement: This story of Lizzie Leek was adapted by Giles Reed from an original idea by Elizabeth Henderson.